STONE BOAT

STONE BOAT

by

Kristen Wittman

TURNSTONE PRESS

Turnstone Press
Artspace Building
607-100 Arthur Street
Winnipeg, MB
R3B 1H3 Canada
www.TurnstonePress.com

Turnstone Press gratefully acknowledges the assistance of The Canada Council for the Arts, the Manitoba Arts Council, the Government of Canada through the Book Publishing Industry Development Program and the Government of Manitoba through the Department of Culture, Heritage and Tourism, Arts Branch, for our publishing activities.

Cover design: Tétro Design
Interior design: Sharon Caseburg

Printed and bound in Canada by Kromar Printing Ltd. for Turnstone Press.

National Library of Canada Cataloguing in Publication Data

Wittman, Kristen, 1972-
        Stone boat / by Kristen Wittman.

Poems.

ISBN 0-88801-296-9

        I. Title.
PS8645.I88S86 2004   C811'.6   C2004-900950-8

to W and A,
who keep me motivated

STONE BOAT

my name is Franklin
i have a story to tell

just the bare bones
lungs
ripped from my chest
throw away your knife and fork and
pick it up
tear into it
chew each bite with the wolf
in your throat

this is the story
of how i learned to remember

***

snapshots
flutter into dusty corners   more
forgotten than remembered
in disarray
and out of order

in order to remember
there is much i must forget

come up with me
into the attic
watch the stairs
don't open that window
i have all my traps up here
everything has been caught
exactly as i want it
look
there is the community hall
with its blue tin roof
the town sign
"A Tradition with a Future"

some days i imagine
lighting a match
and burning it all away

***

i remember my thirteenth birthday
sitting at my desk in long pants
itching at my knees
i was afraid to ask
all year i held my hands at my sides
afraid of snickerings from the bigger boys
in the back row
afraid of the rocks they'd throw
on my way home for lunch

Mother promised me a cake
and Father agreed to a picnic
the lake on sunday he said
and that sweet delicate
twelve-year-old Alice
with blond hair in tight braids
and butterflies in her eyes
thought her family might be going, too

i raise my hand
but the answer is something i know

when i was thirteen the world was smooth
rounded by answers to questions

***

moonshine everywhere
the night my brother died
i went into the cellar
took each jar out
from under the stairs

i
opened them all
there were more than i thought
stashed behind the freezer
i poured them down
one by one
down the big white sink
the bitter smell
like moth balls

***

the prairie
in this photo when i was a child
was dry and unforgiving
death took his place
in shriveled roots
between dried clumps of clay

clouds scraped the edges of the sky
always empty
of promises

still
this photo shows Father
hard work could bring in a crop
to spite the drought

let the snow fly
lay itself out like a blanket
and wait for life to begin again

now death wriggles in the form of slugs
hovers invisible as mosquitoes
on pools of stinking water
drowns the fields
laps at the tractor rusting in the mud
worms into the brains of my cows
creeps closer to my heart

***

i live on Geyser Road
ten miles from Arborg
it's not as pretty as it sounds

it is the seventeenth day of spring
i stand in the snowy water
near the ditch today i am
welcoming the geese
they honk as they return
this is their home too

if you look straight up at the sky
you will see
straight through to the ocean floor
it is the centre of the world

the young men from town
are building a dyke
Lake Winnipeg is ten miles away

still the snow melts
life rushes its way
round my ankles

***

the house in the background
freshly painted red and white
rooted as a hazard marker
shimmering on the surface
of the land

this stony land

Mother must have taken the photo
Father stands with one hand
to my shoulder
anchoring me
i am balancing on the rocks
pitched into the stone boat
during the cool hours of dawn
Karr is dancing on the ground
in front of us
caught in mid-step

i can recall the details of this photo
with my eyes closed
i roll the sense of the place
over on my tongue
feel the farm
lapping against the house

***

goddamn
it's 4 am
my digital flashes red
the only thing i can see
Karr is banging blue streaks in his room
the air around me grainy like newspaper
stumbling down the stairs
i find the switch
light tumbles into my boots
he's already outside
the shotgun
blasting orange against a silent night
while i rub my fists
into my eyes

we wake to a still dawn
outside there are three
dead hens
one mauled, the other two killed
by stray shot
and one rangy red fox
lying in a scarlet pool
as if stained by his fur
the dirt around him moist
in the fall light

***

death is on its way
i can see it
here in my kitchen
Arborite table chipped
wobbles on uneven legs
as i lean to stand

death is in the crabgrass
the rain
the thistle
i have chased Guenther away
i thought he was death
i thought his absence
would save me
my farm
this was my first mistake

the weeds choke the cows
the rotting trees fall
the standing water thickens

it is only a question of time

time stretches its hands into the house
rattles my lungs

***

they sent Guenther's wife over
yesterday
across the fields
apron tucked around her rolling waist
hair pulled tight behind her head
makes a stronger argument
they had told her
i made her some tea
(i hate tea   but with women
you have to   )
the dirt stood out under my nails

Guenther's lug of a brother
has seen a ghost
in his room
needs a new place to stay
she thinks Karr's room would be good
a change for him
blinks her eyelashes
but i won't have that
i will fix up the basement
there's a sink and a separate door
Guenther's wife will pick out the furniture
that never much mattered to me

***

i have lived in this house
all my life
never suffered
the disappointment
of coming home

the crickets do not chase me out
with their senseless twitchings
i feel no need
to search
down gravel roads
following power lines
search with eyes
heavy as an anchor
only to be fixed to
somewhere i once was
and did not remember

***

Billy Creekbed showed me what to do
to snare jackrabbits
he had his own traplines
running out into the fields behind his mother's house
in the wintertime the lines ran
invisible out into an ocean of horizon
the snow rippled
a beach at lowtide
or Lake Winnipeg
caught under a gloomy sky
we checked the lines
blowing hot breath on our frozen fingers

once i saw him chase down a rabbit
that only just jigged the line
breath puffing out of his mouth
sweat crystals on his forehead
he was the wind and the rabbit
jumped up into his hands
neck limp
eyes turned up to the sky

***

you see in this photo
inside the torn edges
Karr and me and Father
standing on the rocks
at the edge of Lake Winnipeg
proudly displaying our catch
the photo has caught
the glint of sunlight
in the dead fish's eye
hanging from my hook

i go there now
wind plays with my hair
and then moves to the water
i pick up fine stones
roll them in my fist
feel the shaping of ancient waters

picture me here
shoulders square
facing out to the lake
watching the pelicans
taking flight
imagine that i
am a man carefree
imagine that
for me

***

this photo is of me
hitching up my overalls
sifting the new feed
Karr went into Gimli
i was working alone
see my hands
those hands are the hands that know
how to keep life simple

the farm is sinking
seeds rising faster than floodwaters
splashing
bursting
popping at me
tireless as machine gun
artillery attack
ripping into my chest

when i awake
Karr shifts in the chair beside me
antiseptic smells of hospital
gunfire inside my lungs

he found me lying on my back
legs swallowed by seed
head on the grass with the dog holding guard
doctor spoke of poison
from the air
said my lungs would never recover
but i was lucky

i was poisoned by mustard fumes
just like my uncles in
the Great War
shrapnel of seeds scarring my lungs

***

i finished school through correspondence
Father took us out in grade ten
to work the fields
i wrote my exams
black thumb
prints on new white paper
mailed them
to some address in Winnipeg
i learned what i had to
and then what i wanted
i have read the Bible
i have read veterinary medicine
i have cured the sick cows

the young vet who comes the rounds these days
studied at the university
but when the old mare
split her neck on the edge of the trailer
his eyes got big like headlights
when i shoved
my fist into the wound
and grabbed hold of the torn jugular
holding tight to ebb the flow
felt the hot blood pulsing
down my arms

while the mare's eyes screamed
he could only gag and puke
hands and knees in the mud and blood

***

last night i dreamt
that Sarge waited until i was asleep
and then ate me

started at my feet and ate his way up
licked my bones smooth
while i tossed under the sheets
then lay back down at the foot of the bed
where he was when i woke up
he looked at me with dopey eyes
panting in his heavy brown coat
i looked deep into those eyes
did he know?

now i keep Sarge's dish full of food
i am all alone and
i can't take any chances

***

here's a photo of me
soldier boy
going off to war   excited
cap crooked to match my grin
she said she loved me
said i looked so dashing in my uniform
i went to Quebec for a year
Karr had to stay home   he had polio and
didn't pass the physical
i drove army trucks
the war ended with a blur of trains
and her death
i'd like to think
she choked on her guilt
but the hospital records said only
she died giving birth
Karr's baby hanged by the cord

the weather was a perfect picture
for a funeral
Karr stood in the cold
rain dripping from his hat
slumped on his cane like an old tree
the wind tugged at the flowers

***

some time passed
before Father sat us down
at the kitchen table
his hands huge and flat on
either side of the placemat
she just started crying one day
eyes hanging inside his head like empty sockets
i want you both to understand
she couldn't remember why
she just couldn't stop crying
she cried herself to death

reached a hand under his chair
placed a brown paper bag on the table
don't start anything you can't finish
knocking his chair back
stomped out of the house

Karr reached for the bag
inside were four squirrels
necks broken
covered in Mother's lipstick

***

i am dying
slowly
i can tell   i can
hear death's footsteps
on the stairs

every night i lie in bed
squeeze each breath
from the rusty old pump
of my lungs
with each jerk and pull
breath drags itself
out of the
bottom of my well

the scuttle of his feet
matches the rhythm of my efforts
his chains beat on the steps
between drags
harsh and echoing

all night sweat pools on my forehead
clings   then
trickles down my temple   onto the pillow
drips like a leaky tap

death waits
by the foot of the stairs
at first
then on the landing
he moves   stealing steps
each breath gets harder to suck
out of the air

in time he moves
with my gurgling breath

***

we made the drive to Thompson
some twenty years ago now
i didn't think then that i would remember
so many details
or that other memories would get pushed aside

i found perspective on that drive
perspective of distance
from the space between two trucks passing
at eighty miles an hour
to the space of three hundred miles
so far you'd think we were in another land
the lake was by our side
for much of the ride
we'd get peeks from between the trees
of its grey slate
like the slip of a shy woman

there were subtle changes
the forests thickened with spruce trees
and the road started rolling
a giant buckled carpet
we were in godless country then
the last church left by the side of the road
just outside the Indian reserve

i learned the perspective of stillness
as the miles clicked the odometer over
uncultivated miles of wilderness
marked only by power lines

and the perspective of time
as we skated over ice-covered highways
at twenty miles an hour
we drove long enough
for the coffee in the thermos
to grow cold

into the darkness
the roads bared themselves to our tires
we watched the line
in the middle disappearing
  into the night
 like a fishing line
into the lake

***

it is only after we have buried him
and i am walking
across the cow pasture
through the forest and i am
following along the creek
a lump forms in my throat

time
is a negative
a photo in a space i no longer recognize
i come upon a neighbouring field
many miles away
i will walk back
along the highway
                    but
    the road
leads in
    the wrong direction

***

Butch moved in three days ago
last night he went down to his room
after dinner and drank
a bottle of vodka
the pitter of mice feet
to keep him company

at 3 am
i thumped down the stairs
shut off the t.v.
he was snoring on his couch
the bottle clutched to his chest
like the locket
of a lover
i turned off the light and climbed back to bed

today he wanted to talk
but i can't listen to the boy
his damn stutter
he said there was a ghost in his bed
at home
said he could see where it slept
when he came home from the fields
it mussed up the sheets
dented his pillow

***

the christmas
when i was eight
Father's brother dressed up as
St. Nicholas
with a big white beard and a red jacket
he was leaving in the new year for Iceland
we kids had no idea it was him
handing out candy canes
he had a present for each of us
and made us line up
and sit on his knee

it was my turn too soon
my hands were sweaty and the ribbon candy
stuck in my throat
he reached down
pulled me onto his lap
and exclaimed what a big smart boy i was
he smelled like liniment
and the box he handed me was
just big enough
to fit the wooden truck
i'd seen in the Eaton's catalogue
i tore open the wrapping

there were leather mitts
to play hockey with
my eyes were too blurred with tears
to see his face
when i threw them into the fire

***

death
is a barnyard activity
see this kitten
full of joy and life
bounces after a ball of string
it doesn't know
tomorrow death will pay its visit
it will take the shape
of a tractor wheel
spinning in the wrong direction
or a draft of wind
slamming a green gate
shut

like the clouds crumpling the sky
any day on the prairie
look up and see

***

Butch found a baby raccoon
tucked under some ferns
brought him home
called him George
he lived with us for almost six months
every morning he'd scratch at the door
if no one let him out
he'd jump up onto the kitchen table
kick plates onto the floor

i heard murmurings
through the kitchen floor
Butch talking to him
with no hitch of stutter
he looked up the stairs
glared at my open mouth

the same look in his eyes
when he held George still with his foot
snapped his neck between his thumbs

***

here's a photo of us in front of the town hall
Karr looked forward to the spring dance
more than anyone i know
he couldn't dance   because of his back
but he would sit and smile and hold his
girl's hand and
bend his head to the music
his laugh rising up like moths from the garden
hit you softly where you stood at the door
i danced
inside
     outside later when it got too hot
         under a blanket of stars and
music seeping from the hall
filling the space
between the stars

back inside i can hardly see him
the lights in my eyes like fireflies
his girl dancing with the doctor's son

in the bathroom
startled as i spin the boy round
urine splashes   knuckles ripping into his cheek
he backs into the sink, buckles his knees
and i wipe my nose on my sleeve
i find a seat next to Karr
my hand pulses to the music
but my feet find no rhythm now

***

i lie awake
waiting for death
who will not come
now that he has me
he teases me, like a lover
leaves me
to search for the secrets
of others

in the silence
i hear the sounds of the ice on the lake
from a distance
crickling and crackling
mice running in a thousand directions

the Icelandic River will flow
for a thousand days
bearing its secrets
over the pebbles
to the lake

***

when Karr got polio
he had to go into hospital
once a week after school
we'd drive to see him in Winnipeg

sometimes Father would stay overnight
making Karr squeeze his hand
over and over
until they both cried
Mother's brow furrowed like storm clouds
so i had to get shots
from a needle as big as a ruler
felt like a bee sting
Mother said
if i was a big boy and didn't cry
i could have a bag of fresh peas
all to myself

***

they dragged him
out behind the rink
one of the older boys with a razor
his arms swung back like a gate
skin the Indian!

i peeked out from behind the warming-up shack
when they let him go Billy ran past me
nicks in his skin and tufts of hair turning pink
he paused and turned
the razor flashed in his eyes

Teacher stood at the front of the class
I demand to know who did this
his face bubbling red   to match the
bloody mass of skinned rabbit on his desk

my hand   frightened barnswallow
raised itself into the air
detention for the rest of the week. Frankly,
I'm surprised at you
i surprised me too
Billy Creekbed's bare head
shone back at me like a beacon

***

it is very late
even Butch
   drunk
      has trembled
into sleep
i have a water glass
filled with whiskey
beside my writing pad
the moon dangles from the sky
ice cold and huge
outside my window
my eyes burn from smoke
off the fields

Father used to call these witching nights
when the wolves cried for hours
he took us outside
our breath ghosting up around us
leaves cracking under our feet
swept his arms
      around
the fields and
       back to us
we must work hard he would say
to keep the wolves away
we must work the fields

the wolves don't want us to survive
so we must always
work harder tomorrow
than we did
today

***

Guenther doesn't listen
i tell him the barn needs painting
the cows need worming
he tells me to go inside
old man he says *old man go inside*
it's too hot for you out here
Butch will turn the fields
go inside
make some tea

sunlight shines a square
onto the kitchen table
i wave my hand through
the motes of light
no blisters
no dirt under the nails

getting old
means having only the memory
of how it feels to be young

***

on saturday
the mercury shriveled into itself
and refused to register
forty below

a stranger was found on sunday
frozen inside his car
a cigarette still in his gloveless fingers
the metal womb
resisted his departure

the prairie will
not allow me to forget
that i am alive

the wind howled much of the night
in the shrill of a saxophone
i covered my ears with my pillow
woke to the silence of its departure

i stick stockinged feet into boots
step onto the porch
in my longjohns
the screen door hangs open
behind me
                the sky
falls in great soft flakes of snow
the size of my hand

***

after Mother died
it was quiet around the house
i learned to cook
and Karr swept the floors the way
Mother had taught us
we stopped going to school
and helped Father with the cows
i had to stand behind the tractor's steering wheel
to plow the back field
the neighbours came over at first
with preserves and bread
they fluttered about the kitchen
chirping and chattering like robins in spring
until Father made it clear
he wanted quiet

when i was twenty-two
we searched all night for him
found him at dawn
slumped against a tree
a few of Mother's pills in his fist
curled up against his chest like a dead spider
his face a frame without a photograph
Karr blinking at me
in the still morning light

***

i thought at first he drank to drown his stutter
drown the dust that floated in his throat
i suppose i
should have looked into his eyes
his stutter only kept the ghosts inside
a lock on a door he couldn't break
even with all his mighty strength
he knew
laughed when i said cabbage moths
splashed vodka onto the table
it's not moths old man

shifting his heft against the creak of the kitchen chair
he sits silent
his fingers flexing around the tumbler

always i thought he was afraid of death
it was the ghosts, old man

***

it is July 21
three days since Karr's death
it has been a slow fuzz
people coming and going
the morning pulls open my eyelids
grainy after each empty night
until the squirrels' clatter
tears through the calm
the smell of death permeates the room
it is my smell now

i am no longer afraid of death
in front of my chipped and warping mirror
i trace my fingers
over the creases
of my face
bare my teeth
to see my skull
lurking inside

if i could reach inside
tear the creases away
expose that grinning skull
dripping with blood and brains

would death take me then?
or would he wait
till my skull was shiny and polished
like a stone
washed by the waves
and spit
onto the shore of Lake Winnipeg

***

Guenther's wife wants to show me
photos of the mountains
i will see how they unfold
toward the sky like giants
with cracked knuckles the sun sets
quickly there slipping behind
the hills lit up like roses
and planes spring suddenly
into the misty sky

i don't look at the pictures
i look out over
the yellow fields
the sky vast as the ocean
i can stand in my fields
this year of canola
and see where i'm going
and where i've been
the world stretches out around me
soft and open as a woman
stretching out on my bed

***

you might think
life is static

but i have lived through a war
watched Father
drown in an ocean of dust
topsoil swirling from the ground

the prairie is not static

i float a raft of wishes
on a sea of wheat
the size of my palm

***

rusty water spills out of the tap
into the can at my feet
every day the cows need water
bucket after bucket
water slops onto the ground
mixing dirt into mud

a photo of Father
leaning into the dirt on his spade
i can see the blisters
popping from his skin
no sign of the secrets
he refused to tell us

death holds no moral ground
is not bound by any rules
i stand in front of my sick cows
and see that now
death is not only stubborn
sitting when you think it will stand
death can be predictable too
death is the small gust of cold
sneaking up your shirt
that is what has made me such a fool

***

i remember long long ago
when i was very small
and Karr and i were playing in the shed
we were climbing on the tractor
where Father kept the gun
and Karr whispered
into my ear

i shot that gun   pulled the trigger just once
to see what would happen
the bullet clanged against the corrugated roof
almost in time with the crackling explosion
Mother came running through the garden
sending moths spraying up into the sky
Karr was laughing

i was proud   i said
i shot that gun
she yelled and cried
and held us both so close
pushed into her breast   almost choking
in the warmth of her embrace
smelling like bread fresh from the oven

***

we must be strong, Franklin
always we must be strong
like the wind
Mother speaks on a day
when the sun will only shine
when no one is looking
leaves on the trees
ringing the range of colours
musical notes
floating to the ground

i am filled like a lung with air
on this autumn day
i am surrounded by pillars of trees
and the lilt of Mother's voice
invisible
its repetitive tune
is all i hear

***

again they send Guenther's wife
she talks about her father
heart attack while shoveling snow
finding him two days later

she worries about me and
Guenther could so easily
do the work
so i tell her i'll try flowers this year
and let the Samuelson boys take over the fields

i go into Gimli
buy peonies
tulips impatiens daisies
i spend hours digging and planting
the impatiens thicken around the trees
grow strong in the shade
to spite the sun
but after all that work
it is the dandelions
shoot up
so bright and constant

***

it is hot
muggy as i imagine
Latin America
not the hot dusty prairie
my water glass sits
in pools of sweat
i look outside the kitchen window
through the slouched trees in the yard
at my cows huddled together
on a dry spot
surrounded by a lake of puddles

the breeze has stopped stirring their manes
and their tails move slower
to flick flies
Butch is working in the fields i know
with his brother
but i hear him still
stomping about in the basement
present as the mice behind the walls

in the cool night i slip out
to the cows
stand inside their circle
the comfort of their tails switching
invisible in the dark
their moist scent
cool and sweet

***

the Samuelson boys promised
they would take care of my cows
spend the days in the fields
playing farmer in their new combines
air-conditioned and computers
no grit under nails
nights they punch VLTs in the bar
swap tales of quotas and holidays over
long empty winters

they forget to fill the tubs
with water there is no
computer to remind them i
carry the buckets out two by two
the handles burning
into my hands blood
sizzling into the snow

***

i shot her

i looked into her sad inky eyes
and she told me
tales of Guenther and Butch
no worming
no feed no water for days
she told me everything
i should have known

then i looked through the sight
to her eye
and shot her
my most beautiful cow
gravity an unbearable knowledge
she moaned
crumpled under her sudden weight
looked up at last to the sky
clouds moving across
the eye of the sun

***

Billy Creekbed
wouldn't go to war
his mother wanted him
to volunteer *be a man*
you're weak as a girl
if the boy waited until conscription
she'd be humiliated
Billy shrugged his shoulders
tossed his ratty hair
pointed at the red gasoline can

his mother gripped him
with white silence

when the mail came
she handed it to Billy
with fire in his eyes
Billy turned to the shed

the gas sprinkled out from the can
standing in the doorway
the match flared
bright flower in his fingers
he could see his mother pull
the drapes in the living room
felt the growing darkness as it
settled on the house like dust

***

i'm not greedy
i'm not needy
don't take me
Christ can't
you see
i've worked so hard
look at me
look at my hands
these hands
every day
keep something
else alive
see my fourth
finger is stubbed
my left thumb
nail black
dirt under my nails
from digging deep
into dirt
keeping the farm
alive with these hands
i will fend you off
dear death
these hands will keep me alive

***

here's a photo
of the cemetery
on the No. 8 highway
they buried Karr
two years ago   not me
                                                    i
wouldn't have done that to him he
told me "cremated" but they knew better
someone always knows better
i walk past the gate
rusted shovel in hand
dig around the tombstone till
          it falls
             heavy but i
                              pick it up again
          let it fall
crack like my spine

my arms won't lift
                    the shovel
          so down to my
knees scrape with my hands
till they bleed
Karr has to
wants to get out

he is screaming
breath without breath like me
can't breathe   a lump in his throat
          vomit everywhere
over the blood and mud
steaming around me   can't breathe
the birds in the sun-stained sky chirp
the lemonsucker sun
so impossibly pinned
to the blue satin sky

***

Gertrude lived above the old hotel pub
on Main Street
in a little pink apartment
painted her fingernails a bright rosy red
and wore lipstick to match
bright smear of red
the men around town always
chipped in when the plumbing broke
i used to meet her at the Chicken Chef
it was liver and onions then
upstairs i had to push
the panties out of the way
just to sit

you sound like a dog
(my wheezy lungs)
she said so i said
let's do it doggie style
(for love i am prepared to abstain
from consequence)
she giggled
her red nails digging
into pink frilly pillows

my thighs banged against her
sweet dimpled bum

my veins exploded
and i howled at the moon
like a wolf

***

flax this year
an ocean full
spreading around me in the
soft dawn light
wild and blue
clouds streaming like
sails in the sky
blood in my lungs
and flax all around
blue as the ocean

blooming thick with blue
everywhere as i stumble
spit blood into the furrows
i drown in this
field of flax

closing over my head
no breath i
can't breathe i
can't   breathe
i am drowning
in my field of flax
waves closing over my head

***

inventory:
12 cows 2 dead
4 sick the
milk gone sour the
light gone
out of their eyes
40 acres
still my own
canary yellow canola
120 acres to Butch and Guenther
120 acres 40   40   40
furrowed flaxed flesh

here are the pictures
they turned to weed
1 homestead peeling paint
a small ship
sinking to the bottom
6 windows with broken seals
back door that won't close
3 scrub oaks 4 ashes 40 feet each
1 creek dry as a sore throat
my farm tearing loose
from its mooring
tossed into the sea

***

there was a time when i
didn't wince from the handles
cutting into my hands
i pour from the cans
into the tub
the cows never notice
splash their noses in the water
step back when i step forward
dump another can's contents

you must understand
death is in every picture

***

this happened to me
my land my house my cows
see what it's like to speak
in a language you don't know
the words
scream out of your lungs
reach inside
take hold of each lung
like the legs of the bleeding calf
pull from the womb
the sound of a boot pulling out of mud
blood squelching between my fingers
knead
your lungs in my hands

twist the air out
like a sponge
until you scream without sound
because no one will hear you
today

today is my reckoning
while spring snow melts into
the mud and blood
i slip and wheeze
until you can see me

take the photo now
take them all now
you can see
                    me
        my lungs throbbing
finally in all this air

this did not happen to me
this is happening to you

***

maybe you will start to understand
if you stand
with legs spread wide
under a prairie sky

clasp your hands
behind your back
and tilt your face
to the sky

watch the clouds sail
on the beautiful blue ocean
of space
feel the motion
in your legs
rock as if
standing in a boat
until you fall

***

then it shall come to this
when my body betrays me
limbs stray and limp
weeds in a soggy pond
now i see
the story my hands
have been telling me
now there will be
no more springs
no seeds
no lilacs scenting the air
until we are dizzy
no renewals
the earth sweats away the winter
but has no place for me
do you see?

i am not a stupid old man
you will be
like me, man
together we will step
into our watery graves
we will see
no more springs

***

my hands float in front of me
my hat flies off my head
my wool pants scratch

like the day Father died
i was sitting all day in church
pants itching my backside
finally, in the outhouse
my feet so far beneath me
not mine
the way the world is
not mine when i look
        at it now
            from above
cars and houses only kids' toys
then dots
my farm a handsome bedspread

i sat in that outhouse
hands on knees and watched
a spider climb the wall and then
string himself down his web to the ground
and scuttle away
i would not have killed him
less regard for me than him
for my new place
here, in the sky
Valhalla   i float   hands like spiders
two more
that got away

***

when Franklin was a little boy
he used to play in his father's fields
in the summer
in the winter
under a sea of sky
and sun he waded through
when he was fourteen

he walked out past the willows
one day deep into the green wheat field
the wheat all around
dizzy with the wind
and under that prairie blue sky
with clouds whipped into aching distance
like sailboats dotting the lake
he began to run
hard his breath pounded through his blood
he ran against the wind
beating his hair off his brow
face blazed by the sun he ran
mouth wide and greedy for air
white moths fluttering around him
batting the air away
he ran and
harsh and loud and deep and throaty
his cry like a wolf
floating up into the wind
softer into the distance

Acknowledgements:

Many thanks to all of the people who supported this project over the years, and in particular: to Clarise Foster, for her kind words and thoughtful comments, and for publishing some of the poems in *CV2*, a very fine journal; to Dennis Cooley, for his time and attention to detail and gentle prodding; to my mother, for listening; to my colleagues at Taylor McCaffrey LLP, for their patience, encouragement and lack of surprise when I claimed to be a poet, too; to Mea, for covering for me while I skipped out to ride my bike through Arborg; to Sharon K. for helping with titles; to Sherry, for her genuine enthusiasm; to Ken, for reading an unbearable first draft (that didn't even rhyme); to Patrick Fitzpatrick, for dragging a starry-eyed articling student along to meet such a fascinating client; and finally, to the farmer who inspired me to write his story, however loosely based.